IMAGES
of America

OCEAN CITY
NEW JERSEY

This map of Ocean City shows the extensive development of the community since its founding. One region that has not seen much development, however, is the area north of Battersea Road (right side), which had only a few homes at the time this map was made. (Senior Studio.)

IMAGES
of America

OCEAN CITY
NEW JERSEY

Frank J. and Robert J. Esposito

ARCADIA

First printed in 1996.
Reprinted in 1998, 2000, 2001, 2002.

Published by Arcadia Publishing,
an imprint of Tempus Publishing, Inc.
2A Cumberland Street
Charleston, SC 29401

Printed in Great Britain.

For all general information contact Arcadia Publishing at:
Telephone 843-853-2070
Fax 843-853-0044
E-Mail sales@arcadiapublishing.com

For customer service and orders:
Toll-Free 1-888-313-2665

Visit us on the internet at http://www.arcadiapublishing.com

*This book is dedicated to John J. and Theresa Esposito,
who dearly loved Ocean City, their family, and each other.*

Contents

Acknowledgments

The authors would like to thank the following individuals and organizations for their assistance in preparing this book: Paul Anselm (president, The Friends of The Ocean City Historical Museum), the staff of the Ocean City Historical Museum, John H. Andrus II (editor, *Ocean City Sentinel-Ledger*), Tom Williams (sports columnist, *Ocean City Sentinel-Ledger*), local historian Harold Lee, Heidi Cuppari, Martha and Tom Gibb, James Lee, Solin Lee, Sue Kasunich Matthews, Nancy Moore, Annetta Jeffries, Mark Soifer (director of public relations for the City of Ocean City), and author Gay Talese. Frederick Herrmann, Peter M. Kalellis, and John R. Taccarino provided guidance and encouragement for this project. Donald Lokuta of Kean College provided technical assistance, and Meg Eberhardt assisted in the preparation of the manuscript.

The authors wish to thank Tara Esposito for her insightful comments and suggestions and Jamie Carter of Arcadia for her superb editorial assistance and support.

We are also very appreciative of the historical background information provided by Doris and Robert Marts of Senior Studio, and their permission to use the marvelous photographs of Al Senior.

Introduction

Founded in 1879 as a "Christian seaside resort," Ocean City, New Jersey, retains its essential charm. It still captures the imagination of countless thousands of loyal vacationers who, on a cold winter's night, dream of a sunny day on its beautiful ocean beaches. It is also a community with a fascinating history.

Originally known as Peck's Beach, so named after John Peck who engaged in whaling here, the 7-mile long island was also used for cattle grazing and for salvaging goods from the many shipwrecks that occurred on its coast. Its first permanent resident was Parker Miller, who lived in a house at Seventh Street and Asbury Avenue which had a kitchen fashioned from the cabin of a shipwrecked vessel. Miller served as a representative for insurance claims for lost cargo and also farmed a bit. In the early days of the community, his house also served as a kind of way station for weary visitors.

The Methodist ministers who founded Ocean City were Reverend Ezra B. Lake, Reverend James B. Lake, Reverend S. Wesley Lake, and Reverend William H. Burrell. Through the Ocean City Association, they created a community where residents and visitors alike could enjoy life in a town governed by religious principles. That they succeeded is best evidenced by two enduring characteristics: the town's still-present ban on the sale of alcoholic beverages and its enduring focus on serving as a family-oriented resort.

Ocean City's best known historic site is at Sixteenth Street and the beach, where the remains of the steel-hulled, four-masted barque *Sindia* still lie beneath the sands. A good part of the ship's cargo, now valued at more than $1,000,000, remains in its buried frame.

The *Sindia* came aground at 1:30 am on December 15, 1901, in a howling storm. The ship continues to grace the postcards of vacationers, as it has for most of this century, and to stir the imaginings of those who wonder what is still in its hold. One persistent legend is that the *Sindia*'s ill-fated voyage from Kobe, Japan, to New York City was star-crossed by the presence of a large 2-ton statue of Buddha on board. To some who believe the story, the relocation of the religious object from its native land brought with it a curse that caused the destruction of the ship. The ship's manifest did not specifically list a large Buddha. However, more than one thousand cases of "curios" are still believed to exist in the buried hull of the ship.

Ocean City is well-known both for its shipwrecks and as home for a large number of famous people. Most notable among these is the Kelly family of Philadelphia—a family still revered on the island. Actress Grace Kelly, later Princess Grace of Monaco, vacationed here as a child with her family and even visited after she became a princess. Her brothers and sisters likewise shared a love of the resort, and Kelly family members still live in the community.

Ocean City also has in its midst one of the finest writers in America—Gay Talese, who still maintains a residence here while also living in New York City. Talese, whose parents operated an Asbury Avenue tailor shop for many years, is the author of several books that have made the *New York Times'* bestseller list, including *Honor Thy Father, The Kingdom and Power, Thy Neighbor's Wife,* and *Unto the Sons.* Five years ago, the New Jersey Literary Hall of Fame inducted Talese.

Ocean City is also a place of picturesque landmarks, a well-kept main street called Asbury Avenue, and a historic district consisting of wonderful Victorian era homes. Its city hall and the Music Pier are both important architectural and historic sites. Unfortunately, some of the best landmarks are gone: the Parker Miller House, Watson's Restaurant, Jernee Manor, Chris' Restaurant, and Hogate's Restaurant. All of these are chronicled here, as well as the many remaining attractions of this unique seaside community.

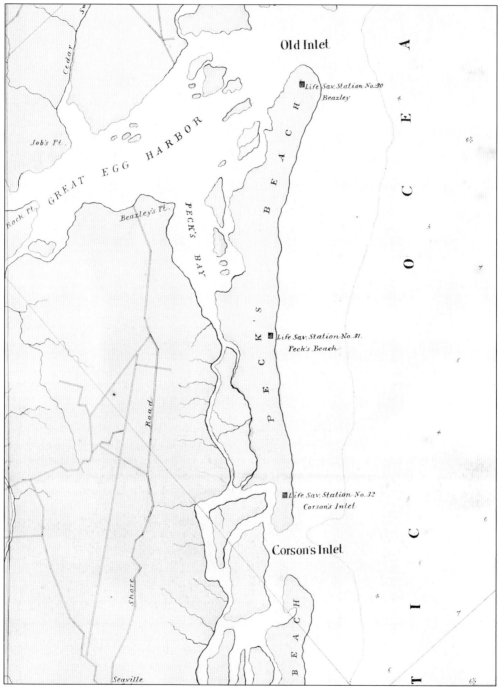

PECK'S BEACH IN 1878. This map, printed in 1878, depicts Peck's Beach one year before it was renamed Ocean City. Note that there are no roads leading to the island from Shore Road, the main highway on the mainland. However, Peck's Beach had three life-saving stations at this time. Station Number 32 was at the southern end of the island at Corson's Inlet, Station Number 31 was in the middle of the island, and Station Number 30 was at the northern end, called "Beazley" on this map.

One
Early History

REVOLUTIONARY WAR CANNON. This Revolutionary War cannon stood on tabernacle grounds for many years at the corner of Sixth Street and Atlantic Avenue. It was taken from the British ship *Delight*, which sunk off the island in 1779 during the Revolutionary War. It was stolen in the 1960s and has not yet been recovered. (Senior Studio.)

PARKER MILLER HOUSE. Parker Miller was the first known permanent resident of Peck's Beach (now Ocean City). Miller served as the agent for marine insurance companies, protecting the companies' interests when ships were wrecked off the island's beaches. He also engaged in raising cattle and farming. His original home site was at Seventh Street and Asbury Avenue. The house depicted here was located at 730 Asbury Avenue, later the location of Woolworth's.

Miller won election to the local council in 1884 and served until 1886. Born in Absecon in 1825, he died in 1901. He is buried in Seaside Cemetery in Palermo, New Jersey, on the mainland only a few miles from Ocean City. (Senior Studio.)

Association House

Ocean City, New Jersey

OPENS JULY 1st and CLOSES SEPT. 1st

FIRST CLASS TABLE

GOOD BEDS   AIRY ROOMS

ELECTRIC LIGHTS

GOOD SANITARY ARRANGEMENTS

Rooms and Table Board, July [double bed], **$6.50**
"   "   " Aug.   " **$7.00**
"   "   " July [single bed], **$8.00**
"   "   " Aug.   " **$8.50**

Location : Facing the Beautiful Grounds of the Auditorium

ASSOCIATION HOUSE ADVERTISEMENT. Many early visitors who came to Ocean City stayed at the Association House, which was located at Sixth Street and Asbury Avenue. It was a short walk from the house to religious services in the tabernacle building. (Senior Studio.)

TABERNACLE TREE. Under this tree, on September 10, 1879, Ocean City was founded by Reverend Ezra B. Lake, Reverend James B. Lake, Reverend S. Wesley Lake, and Reverend William H. Burrell. The Honorable Simon Lake and Reverend William B. Wood later joined them in incorporating the association. (F.J. Esposito.)

TABERNACLE TREE (MARKER). This tree, which is traditionally associated with the founders of Ocean City, once stood near North Street but was later moved to the tabernacle grounds. (F.J. Esposito.)

ARTIST PAINTING TABERNACLE. In this mid-century photograph an artist paints a picture of the original tabernacle building, located between Fifth and Sixth Streets near Atlantic Avenue. The wooden structure was replaced in 1957 in order to make way for the present, modern tabernacle building. (Senior Studio.)

POSTCARD OF THE TABERNACLE, 1906. The original Ocean City Tabernacle, or Auditorium as it was also called, is depicted in this 1906 postcard.

The Auditorium, Ocean City, N. J.

POSTCARD OF THE TABERNACLE, *c.* 1910. As with similar auditoriums in religious communities, such as those in Pitman, New Jersey, the Ocean City Tabernacle stood at the center of many pathways leading to it.

END OF SUNDAY SERVICES. Worshippers are shown leaving the tabernacle building after Sunday services, *c.* 1950. The tabernacle attracted many famous speakers over the years, including Norman Vincent Peale.

THE TABERNACLE BUILDING TODAY. The modern tabernacle building continues to be a hub of summertime activity with a popular program of services and nationally-known speakers.

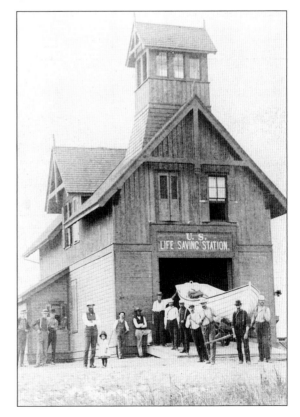

LIFE SAVING STATION NUMBER 67. Built in 1893, Life Saving Station Number 67 likely replaced the Station Number 30 indicated on the 1878 map of Peck's Beach. This station at Fourth Street and Atlantic Avenue is now in use as a private residence. (Senior Studio.)

STEAMBOAT WHARF. Steamboat service from Longport to Ocean City began in 1894 and lasted until 1918. Four steamboats called *Avalon*, *Longport*, *Wildwood*, and *Somers Point* moved passengers across the bay and inlet. In 1903 the line earned a profit of $6,000, but its income declined after the opening of the Shore Fast Trolley line (which ran to the mainland) in 1907. By 1919 the steamboat line ceased operations. (Senior Studio.)

THE STEAMBOAT *SOMERS POINT*. The steamer *Somers Point* arrives at the Second Street wharf with a boatload of visitors to Ocean City. This postcard was mailed from Atlantic City on July 3, 1911.

Two
Community

BOURSE BUILDING. Asbury Avenue was the first street opened in Ocean City. It remains the most important street for commercial business activity and for parades. Pictured here is the Bourse Building, which is still standing at the northeast corner of Eighth Street and Asbury Avenue. For many years, the Bourse Building was the location of Murphy's Five and Ten Cent Store; upstairs was the office of a local dentist, Dr. Homer Gerkin. (Senior Studio.)

ADAMS/PENLAND STORE. Mrs. T. Lee Adams and son stand in front of their fishing tackle store on the northwest corner of Seventh Street and Asbury Avenue. The magnificent building continues to be operated as a store called Penland Place, and is owned by civic leader James Penland. (Senior Studio.)

POWELL'S MARKET PARADE FLOAT. Powell's Market, located between Seventh Street and Eighth Street on Asbury Avenue, sponsored a float in this early-twentieth-century view. (Senior Studio.)

JOHN C. GANDY GROCERIES. John C. Gandy operated a grocery business at 745 Asbury Avenue. He delivered goods around town with a horse-drawn wagon, as shown in this early-twentieth-century photograph. (Senior Studio.)

ADAMS STORE. The store of George O. Adams at 715 Asbury Avenue is shown here c. 1915.

THORN STORE. The R. Howard Thorn building at 801 Asbury Avenue appears here in the early 1900s. A bank building later occupied the site. (Senior Studio.)

HARDWARE STORE. A close-up of the hardware store at 801 Asbury Avenue is featured in this *c.* 1900 photograph.

EIGHTH STREET AND ASBURY AVENUE. By 1913, about when this photograph was taken, the automobile seemed well on its way to replacing the horse-drawn wagon. The corner of Eighth Street and Asbury Avenue remains today as one of the city's busiest. The Men's Shop on the left, opened in 1913, was operated by Howard S. Stainton. Stainton built a large commercial empire that also included real estate development and fuel oil distribution. He built a new store on the site in 1941 and expanded it in 1961. (Senior Studio.)

ASBURY AVENUE, 1930. The two stores in the left center of this 1930 photograph formed the basis of Stainton's Department Store. Even in his later years, Howard S. Stainton continued to greet customers in his Asbury Avenue department store. Stainton was a wonderful benefactor who gave much to the community. He donated a chapel and pipe organ to the local United Methodist Church, and land for the Wesley Manor retirement home as well as for a senior citizen center at Thirty-third Street and Bay Avenue. (Senior Studio.)

ASBURY AVENUE, 1949. This 1949 view of Asbury Avenue shows the three-story Stainton's Department Store on the far side of the street. Note Warren's, Senior Studio, and the Gulf gasoline station on the same side of the street. These three buildings are still standing. The gas station is now used for business offices. (Senior Studio.)

JOHNSTONE'S RESTAURANT. Johnstone's Restaurant was a popular establishment at 856 Asbury Avenue. The building now houses the Spinning Wheel Florist, which is operated by City Councilman Mark Videtto. (Senior Studio.)

CHATTERBOX. The Chatterbox has for decades been a popular Ocean City restaurant and landmark. The Spanish style structure is on the southeastern corner of Ninth Street and Central Avenue. This postcard is from the early 1960s.

Watson's

RESTAURANT

OCEAN AVE. at NINTH

SINCE 1934

OPEN MID—MAY THRU MID—SEPTEMBER

SERVING DINNERS DAILY

MODERATE PRICES
CHILDREN'S MENU
FREE PARKING
GIFT SHOP
500 SEATS

WATSON'S RESTAURANT. Watson's Restaurant at the corner of Ninth Street and Ocean Avenue was a famous local establishment. Lines of customers waiting for tables frequently spilled out onto Ocean Avenue during the summer months. The restaurant building was demolished several years ago and Watson's Regency Suites now occupies the site.

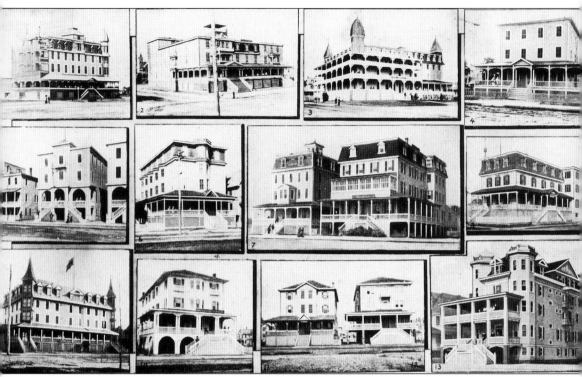

OCEAN CITY HOTELS, c. 1915. The Ocean City hotels featured in this promotional brochure are shown as they appeared to early-twentieth-century visitors. Most early-twentieth-century visitors to Ocean City apparently stayed at one of these hotels. The rates were usually reasonable and the beach nearby. Sadly, most are gone today with fire being a frequent cause of their demise.

FLANDERS HOTEL. The Flanders Hotel at Eleventh Street and Boardwalk was built in 1922-23 in Mission Revival style at a cost of one and one-half million dollars. The impressive hotel had an initial capacity of over two hundred rooms. This is a 1920s postcard view. Fortunately, the building has survived to the present.

FLANDERS POOL. The salt water pools at the Flanders Hotel attracted many customers until the pool complex was torn down a decade or so ago. Today, the former pool site contains an amusement park.

NORMANDIE HOTEL. The Normandie Hotel is here shown with the beach in front of it at Ninth Street and Ocean Avenue prior to the construction of the first boardwalk. This view is *c.* 1912.

NORMANDIE HOTEL. The Normandie Hotel was a very popular vacation home for countless Ocean City visitors. It is shown here *c.* 1920s. It was destroyed in the 1927 fire.

HOTEL DELAWARE. The majestic Hotel Delaware, on Third Street, is pictured here in a 1941 postcard view.

LINCOLN HOTEL. The Lincoln Hotel, pictured here in the late 1920s or 1930s, was located at Ninth Street and Wesley Avenue.

CENTRAL AVENUE, 1907. Central Avenue rooming houses are shown in this 1907 postcard. The view is from Fourteenth Street looking northward toward Thirteenth Street.

WESLEY AVENUE, c. 1915-20. This vintage photograph of a virtually empty Wesley Avenue, taken around 1915 to 1920, shows the original trolley tracks that ran in the center of the street.

MOWBRAY. In addition to the large hotels, smaller rooming houses and bed-and-breakfast establishments accommodated many visitors. The Mowbray at Tenth Street and Central Avenue is pictured here in this 1938 postcard.

MOORLYN VIEW. The Moorlyn View rooming houses at 816-820 Ocean Avenue offered "running water in all rooms," according to this c. 1940 postcard. The Moorlyn View at the foot of Moorlyn Terrace was operated by the Moore family. (N. Moore/Mowen Studio.)

TRAIN STATION, c. 1902. The train station at Tenth Street and Haven Avenue was only about two years old when this photograph was taken. Rail service to Ocean City from Tuckahoe (and later from Philadelphia) began in the 1880s and ran until 1981. This well-restored station is on the National Register of Historic Places and is currently used as a transportation center for buses. (Senior Studio.)

TRAIN STATION, 1954. A Pennsylvania Reading Seashore Line engine is pictured here in 1954 at the Tenth Street and Haven Avenue Train Station. This engine picked up passengers at Tuckahoe from the Cape May Express. (Senior Studio.)

"YELLOW KID." Many hotel visitors came to Ocean City by train. The "Yellow Kid," pictured here c. 1890, ran from Stone Harbor to Ocean City from 1889 until 1934. (Senior Studio.)

FIRST AIRMAIL FLIGHT. One of the first airmail flights in the United States took place between Stone Harbor and Ocean City between August 3 and August 10, 1912. The flight was part of a federal plan for experimental airmail delivery in sixteen states. Pictured here are pilot Marshall Earl Reid and Edna Bramell. Bramell was the first woman passenger on one of the exhibition flights that followed the original historic trip. During the initial flight, Reid's mechanic Orton Hoover also piloted the hydroplane. The flight from Stone Harbor to Ocean City—with a landing on the beach—took twenty-nine minutes. (Senior Studio.)

LAYING OF CITY HALL CORNERSTONE, 1914. Mayor Harry Headley presided over these ceremonies on Easter Sunday 1914 for the laying of the cornerstone for city hall at Ninth Street and Asbury Avenue.

CITY HALL DEDICATION, 1914. Built by John W. Emery of Philadelphia, the Ocean City City Hall officially opened on January 1, 1915, with hundreds of local residents touring the building. The total cost of the building was approximately $76,000, considered a bargain by many at the time although some townspeople felt even this expenditure too excessive. This view is also of the 1914 dedication ceremony.

CITY HALL. City hall originally served as the town's administrative, fire, and police department headquarters. Today, it is used for city administrative offices only. The larger photograph above shows city hall under construction in 1914, and the inset depicts the building today. At one time there was a goldfish pond on the Ninth Street side of the building. The temperance water fountain remains at the Ninth Street corner.

OCEAN CITY HIGH SCHOOL DEDICATION. The new Ocean City High School, housed in a beautiful brick building between Fifth and Sixth Streets and Ocean and Atlantic Avenues, was dedicated in these 1924 ceremonies.

DIRIGIBLE *AKRON* OVER HIGH SCHOOL. The United States dirigible *Akron* was photographed in 1932 as it passed over the high school. Approximately one year later, on April 4, 1933, this airship—the world's largest—crashed in the ocean off the New Jersey coast near Little Egg Inlet. Seventy-two of seventy-six crew members were lost. (Senior Studio.)

OCEAN CITY HIGH SCHOOL. The impressive front entrance to Ocean City High School is shown here before it was renovated and redesigned. The high school building, which is still in use, formally opened in 1924; the first graduation was held a year later. (Senior Studio.)

OCEAN CITY TEACHERS, *c.* 1955. Ocean City teachers and administrators gather for a meeting in the early to mid-1950s. Among those in attendance are George W. Myers (high school principal) and Berwyn Hughes (elementary school teacher and later principal). Speaking to the group is Kenneth Landis, principal of the Central Avenue Elementary School. In addition to the Central Avenue School, built on the site of an earlier school, older Ocean City schools also included the Wesley Avenue School, now the Lake Memorial Park. The former Central Avenue School now serves as the police and safety headquarters. (*Ocean City Sentinel-Ledger.*)

THE CAREY BROTHERS. T. John Carey (center) and Fenton Carey (right), pictured here with their brother Lewis, both served as outstanding Ocean City High School coaches. T. John Carey is also acknowledged as one of the pioneers of surfing on the East Coast. Carey Stadium is named after T. John and Fenton. (Senior Studio.)

OCHS GIRLS' BASKETBALL TEAM, 1926. The 1926 Ocean City High School girls' basketball team is featured here. Second from the left is Miriam Reichley, who had a long career as a coach of girls' sports.

COACH "DIXIE" HOWELL AND THE 1956-57 BOYS' BASKETBALL TEAM. Ocean City High School Coach Fred "Dixie" Howell is an almost legendary figure on the island. Regarded by many as one of the finest high school basketball coaches in the state and nation, "Dixie" Howell's teams won two state championships and many south Jersey titles. Pictured here with Howell is the 1956-57 team, which was undefeated in the regular season; the team lost to Verona in the state championship finals.

OCEAN CITY DOCTORS, 1925. Ocean City doctors in 1925 included, from left to right: (front row) John B. Townsend, Hershel Pettit, Allen Corson, and Aldrich Crowe; (back row) Willetts Haines, John H. Whiticar, Marcia V. Smith, and G. Eugene Darby.

DR. MARCIA V. SMITH MONUMENT. Dr. Marcia V. Smith became the first woman physician in Ocean City in 1922. This monument to her was dedicated on October 6, 1960, as part of "Marcia Smith Week" in Ocean City. The monument was erected in recognition of Smith's assistance in the creation of the nation of Israel. Dr. Smith, who died in 1995, was, along with James Penland, one of the founders of the Boardwalk Art Show. She was married to Chris Montagna, who owned and operated Chris' Restaurant.

EARLY OCEAN CITY MAILMEN. These early Ocean City postmen, *c.* 1905, took obvious pride in their uniforms and their work. The United States Post Office authorized mail carrier service for Ocean City in 1902. The first post office, located on Eighth Street, operated until 1910 when a new building opened between Asbury Avenue and Central Avenue on the same street.

OCEAN CITY POST OFFICE. The current Ocean City Post Office, pictured here, began serving customers in 1937 and is still in use.

ST. PETER'S UNITED METHODIST CHURCH. The first church established in Ocean City was the Methodist church, which reflected the religion of the community's founders. The first Methodist church services were conducted by Reverend Ezra B. Lake, one of the city's founders, and held in the Association Hall at Seventh Street and Asbury Avenue. Pictured above is the stone church built in 1906 at Eighth Street and Central Avenue; the building is still in use as St. Peter's United Methodist Church. (F.J. Esposito.)

ST. AUGUSTINE'S ROMAN CATHOLIC CHURCH. St. Augustine's Roman Catholic Church dates to 1894. This building on Asbury Avenue near Fourteenth Street served as the main parish until the 1931 construction of a spacious brick church at Thirteenth Street and Wesley Avenue.

ST. JOHN'S LUTHERAN CHURCH. Organized in 1923, St. John's Lutheran Church was moved by parishioners from Woodlawn, New Jersey, in 1924 and reassembled on the southeast corner of Tenth Street and Central Avenue. The building has been renovated and expanded several times since then. (F.J. Esposito.)

TABERNACLE BAPTIST CHURCH. Founders moved this building to Eighth Street and West Avenue in 1908. It previously stood at Eighth Street and Central Avenue, where it first served as a Methodist church. The Baptist church organization itself dates to 1896, when parishioners held their first meetings in the Knights of Pythias Hall at Seventh Street and Asbury Avenue, thereby making it the oldest African-American congregation in Ocean City. (F.J. Esposito.)

"HOBO." Found in a snowdrift in 1920, Hobo became a popular local figure who also received nationwide publicity. Some residents recall that he used to lie in the middle of the boardwalk in summer and was fed so frequently by passers-by that he became rotund. This photograph shows Hobo in 1936, the eighteenth and final year of his life. (Senior Studio.)

HOBO FOUNTAIN. The Hobo Fountain at Twelfth Street and Wesley Avenue remains as a reminder of Ocean City's mascot. When the town's mascot died in 1936 at age eighteen, local residents erected this fountain with a lower level for dogs in his honor. It first stood in front of the high school building, but is now at the Ocean City Historical Museum's Seashore Cottage at Twelfth Street and Wesley Avenue. (F.J. Esposito.)

COLUMBUS CLUB INSTALLATION DINNER. Ocean City's Italian-American community formed the Columbus Club early in the twentieth century. The club was originally called the Italian Independent Club when it was incorporated in October 1921. The name was formally changed to Columbus Club in February 1942 during the early years of World War II. The club, located at 927 Simpson Avenue, served as an active social organization for many decades. The

Italian-American community was a close-knit one with many families emigrating to America from the same Italian villages. In Ocean City they frequently settled on the same street as their fellow villagers. Pictured here are members and guests attending a January 1951 installation dinner. Note the American flags covering the side walls of the club. The building is still standing and is in use as a church.

MISS DIAMOND JUBILEE. Marla Adams served as Miss Diamond Jubilee Queen in the 1954 celebration of the 75th anniversary of Ocean City's founding. Here the stunning queen poses with her crown and scepter. (Senior Studio.)

Three
Boardwalk and Beach

BOARDWALK SCENE. This mid-twentieth-century scene shows a busy Ocean City promenade. Shrivers Store, on the left in this photograph, is believed to be the oldest on the boardwalk.

BROWER'S BATHS. Brower's Baths offered a little bit of everything to visitors, including shuffleboard and target shooting as well as a place to shower and change.

OCEAN CITY BOARDWALK. The Ocean City boardwalk is shown here in a 1905 postcard view. This boardwalk was located much further inland than the present one.

CREOLE DONUT SHOP. The Creole Donut Shop was located at 928 Boardwalk before the 1927 fire. This 1920s photograph is similar to those done by Walker Evans and other WPA (Works Progress Administration) photographers a decade later. (Senior Studio.)

BEAUTY CONTEST. This beauty contest, which took place *c.* 1925, was held in front of the 900 block of the old boardwalk. Faunce's Theatre can be seen in the rear of the photograph. (Senior Studio.)

Public Music Pavilion & Pier,
Ocean City, N. J.

MUSIC PAVILION (CONVENTION HALL). Convention Hall was also known as the Music Pavilion when it stood on the ocean side of the pre-1928 boardwalk. This location undoubtedly helped it escape being destroyed in the 1927 fire, which burned most of the boardwalk. The building was then moved to Sixth Street and Boardwalk, where it served as a focal point for dances and basketball. However, fire consumed the structure in 1965.

Music Pavilion at night, Ocean City, N. J.

MUSIC PAVILION (CONVENTION HALL) AT NIGHT. This 1907 artist's rendering exaggerated the size of the Music Pavilion (Convention Hall).

48

HIPPODROME. The Hippodrome at Ninth Street and Boardwalk is pictured here before 1927. (Senior Studio.)

PERKINS AND DARBY. Popular baritone Tom Perkins is accompanied here by Jeanette Darby, Miss New Jersey of 1925, in a musical duet c. 1930. Perkins sang at the Music Pier for many decades and also operated a boardwalk store for many years.

MUSIC PIER AND BOARDWALK, 1943. This half-century-old view shows the moonlit Music Pier and boardwalk in 1943. Note Simms' Restaurant on the left. The Simms' building is now an arcade.

MUSIC PIER TODAY. The Spanish Revival building continues to serve as a focal point for cultural and civic activities. Constructed in 1928-29 after the 1927 fire, the pier has survived many storms and hurricanes with its beauty intact. (F.J. Esposito)

PLAYLAND AND BOARDWALK. The Playland Amusement Complex at Sixth Street and Boardwalk is shown here c. 1930. (Senior Studio.)

PLAYLAND SKATING RINK, 1940s. Playland offered many enjoyable diversions. Here skaters enjoy the indoor rink in the early 1940s.

PLAYLAND BOWLING ALLEY, 1940. Bowling was a popular activity at Playland. The alleys had polished wood floors and ample space in which to bowl. This view is from February 1940.

GILLIAN'S FUN DECK, *c.* 1950s. Plymouth Place was the site of great fun for children. They could ride a Ferris wheel and enjoy other amusements.

BINGHAM'S KIDDIE RIDES. Located at Eleventh and Boardwalk, this business has now been renamed Playland by its owners, but it was not connected with the Playland at Sixth Street and Boardwalk that was destroyed by fire in 1961.

MOORLYN THEATRE NEWS TEAM. The Moorlyn Theatre, located at Boardwalk and Moorlyn Terrace, has been an Ocean City landmark for many years. (Mowen.)

SOUTHEND BOARDWALK. Few people realize that there once was a southend boardwalk. This wooden walkway extended for about two blocks, running north from Fifty-eighth Street.

FIFTY-NINTH STREET PIER. The Fifty-ninth Street Pier was a popular haven for fishermen and tourists. This view is from 1936. Only the ocean side of the pier is now standing, with the deck missing on much of the remaining part. The future use of the pier is still somewhat in doubt. (Senior Studio.)

Bathing Hour, Ocean City, N. J.
K. M. Jereissati, Publisher.

I'd like a row very much. Wouldn't you like a bath? Perhaps a sail would suit you better. D.M.

BATHING HOUR, 1906. Victorian bathers took to the beach with ample sunscreen protection, as this postcard reveals. On this card, "D.M." wrote to "Winifred" in Waterford, New Jersey, that, "I'd like a row very much. Wouldn't you like a bath?" This August 27, 1906, message obviously referred to one of the much-used boardwalk bathhouses.

On the Beach, Ocean City, N. J.

Here with a crowd of girls. Having a dandy time. Grace

MORRISTOWN, N.J.
JUL 4 1 - PM

ON THE BEACH, 1906. Despite the Victorian-era bathing suits, these beachgoers appear to be enjoying the surf and the sand in 1906. On this July 3 postcard, "Grace" wrote to "Sarah" that she was "here with a crowd of girls having a dandy time." Grace mailed the postcard to her friend in Newark, but it was forwarded to Morristown. Hopefully Sarah got the message.

FLANDERS HOTEL AND BEACH, *c.* 1935. Bathers gather in 1935 on the Eleventh Street beach. The Flanders Hotel looms majestically in the background. Also shown is the new boardwalk that replaced the one destroyed in the 1927 fire. (Senior Studio.)

TWO BATHERS, SIXTEENTH STREET BEACH, *c.* 1902. Two Victorian-era beachgoers use an umbrella to write in the sand.

Ocean City Life Guards, Ocean City, N. J.

EARLY OCEAN CITY LIFEGUARDS. Officially created in 1920, Ocean City's Beach Patrol is considered by many people to be among New Jersey's finest. At the turn of the century, these pre-Beach Patrol lifeguard uniforms appeared a bit uncomfortable.

BEACH TENT. This beach tent was at Tenth Street *c.* 1948.

OCBP HEADQUARTERS AT TENTH STREET. The picturesque Ocean City Beach Patrol Headquarters at Tenth Street withstood many a northeaster until the March 1962 Storm washed it away. Here it is shown in the 1950s. (Senior Studio.)

OCEAN CITY BEACH PATROL. The Ocean City Beach Patrol is shown *c.* 1940 at the Tenth Street beach with Captain Jack Jernee (on the right in a white suit) and Dr. Marcia V. Smith (in white on left). From 1949 to 1978 the beach patrol won or tied twenty out of thirty South Jersey Lifeguard Championships.

WARD BEAM'S GIRLS. This photograph of "Ward Beam's Girls" dates from the mid-1920s. Ward Beam was one of the leaders of beach exercise at that time. (Senior Studio.)

BEACH EXERCISE CLASS. This exercise class enjoyed beach activities as some spectators watched from the shade under the boardwalk in 1925. (Senior Studio.)

BEACH SCENE, 1921. This 1921 beach scene shows young people having a good time on the beach in front of the old boardwalk establishments of Faunce's Theatre and Goff's Baths.

GENERAL VIEW OF BATHING BEACH, 1935. The vacationer sending this card commented: "It's really <u>grand</u> down here and am having a perfectly <u>grand</u> time." The unsigned message also gave the standard greeting: "Wish you were here."

BEACH SCENE. These boys and girls are enjoying making sand castles in this early-twentieth-century view. (Senior Studio.)

SECOND STREET BEACH, 1939. Bathers and umbrellas crowd the beach at Second Street in this 1939 photograph.

BOYS ON BEACH WHERE EIGHTH AND OCEAN AVENUES MEET TODAY. These boys are huddled on the beach in front of the pre-1927 boardwalk, which was destroyed by fire. They would be sitting at the intersection of Eighth Street and Ocean Avenue today. (Senior Studio.)

OCEAN CITY BEACH SCENE, c. 1940s. A dozen young men and women gather in front of a lifeguard boat for a picture in the 1940s. (Senior Studio.)

BEACH SCENE, 1922. On this postcard (postmarked July 20, 1922), "Helen" wrote to "Charles" that, "we are having a good time and as usual I am fairly well sunburn't."

BEACH IN GARDENS, 1955. A crowded beach in the Gardens section of Ocean City is shown here in the 1950s. Note the beach patrol headquarters in the rear center of the photograph and the Atlantic City skyline in the distance.

FISHERMAN WITH SHARK, 1916. This dramatic pose of a fisherman with a huge shark dates back to 1916. Although this fisherman stands proudly behind the shark, it is unclear whether the shark was actually caught in the surf, at sea, or if it just washed ashore. (Senior Studio.)

WHALE ASHORE, 1929. On May 3, 1929, spectators viewed a 58-ton whale measuring 62 feet that washed ashore.

Four
Bayfront Landmarks

FORMER CHRIS' RESTAURANT SITE. These buildings are some of only a few original buildings remaining from the Chris' Restaurant site at Ninth Street and Palen Avenue on the bayfront. The Dockside Cafe now also occupies part of the former Chris' property. (F.J. Esposito.)

BOAT RAMP AND SHED. This boat ramp and boathouse, dating from the 1890s and owned by Martha and Tom Gibb, is located at Eleventh Street and Bay Avenue. It is the only known boathouse structure surviving unchanged from the late nineteenth century.

BAYFRONT AT FOURTH AND BAY. Allen's at Fourth Street and Bay Avenue was a popular spot for the departures and arrivals of fishing parties. Here, in 1949, the *Peerless* returned to port with seven people aboard.

OLD BOATHOUSE, ELEVENTH STREET AND BAYFRONT. This is an old photograph of another boathouse at Eleventh Street and the bayfront. The building has been remodeled but still survives as a reminder of the past. (A. Jeffries.)

BOATHOUSE AND BOATYARD. The rear of the remodeled boathouse faced the former boatyard of the marina operated by Anthony Capeza for many years. A condominium now occupies the site of the marina. (A. Jeffries.)

OCEAN CITY YACHT CLUB. The Ocean City Yacht Club on Battersea Road and the bayfront is pictured here in 1923. The spacious clubhouse fell victim to spiraling upkeep costs and was torn down. (Senior Studio.)

PENNSYLVANIA RAILROAD CLUBHOUSE. This photograph of the Pennsylvania Railroad Clubhouse at Second Street and the bay was taken in 1910. (Senior Studio.)

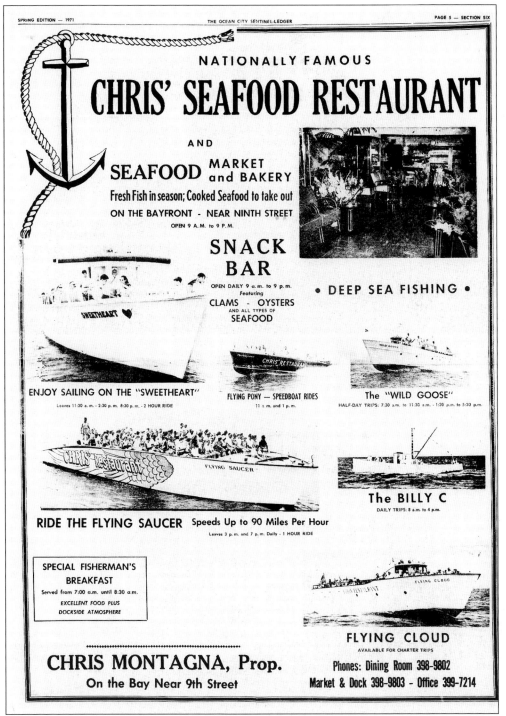

ADVERTISEMENT FOR CHRIS' RESTAURANT. This 1971 advertisement for the popular Chris' Restaurant (located between Ninth and Tenth Streets on Palen Avenue) reveals some of the attractions of this landmark establishment. Sadly, most of the property faced the wrecker's ball less than a decade later.

CHRIS' RESTAURANT, EARLY 1950s. This Senior Studio photograph of Chris' Restaurant depicts it at the height of its popularity. Chris Montagna and his wife, Dr. Marcia V. Smith, developed the restaurant and fish market into a famous local attraction. Chris, also known as "Captain Chris," was a charismatic showman who knew how to attract the public. Chris, who almost always dressed in an immaculate white uniform, knew that most people wanted a "thrill ride" over the ocean, so he worked with the Holtz family to build the *Flying Saucer* and other speedboats. He also operated fishing boats and offered a more sedate sailboat cruise on the *Sweetheart*.

CHRIS' SEA FOOD MARKET   916 Palen Avenue
Ocean City, New Jersey
398-9803

COVER OF 1960S MENU. This is the cover of a 1960s menu that featured the *Flying Saucer* speedboat. Patrons could dine in the restaurant or the seafood market as well as at dockside on the bayfront.

CHRIS' SEA FOOD MARKET

CLAMS On Half Shell .... $ .70
COCKTAILS—Shrimp 1.25
      Crabmeat 1.25
      Lobster 1.50
SOUP—Clam Chowder .... .55
      Snapper Soup .... .60

★

PLEASE PAY WHEN SERVED

★

LARGE PLATTERS

Platters include Tartar Sauce and Cole Slaw
Choice of French Fries or Potato Salad

1—ASSORTED SEA FOOD $2.00
2—FRIED OYSTERS (4) 1.75
3—DEVILED CRAB 1.65
4—DEVILED CLAM 1.50
5—SHRIMP (5) 1.80
6—SCALLOPS (8) 1.60
7—SOFT SHELL CRAB 1.80
8—SCALLOPS (4) and SHRIMP (3) 1.70
9—FLOUNDER 1.60

PIE	30c	COFFEE	15c	
CAKE	25c	TEA	~~15c~~ 20	
		MILK	~~15c~~ 20	

WILL
Deep Sea Fishing -
Join Ride in Afterno

FLYIN
Thrill Ride Starting
1

FLYIN
For a Thrill Ride -
5200 Horsepower -
1

SWEETHE
Leave 11:30 A.M.
1½ to

FLYIN
8:30 A.

"B
DEEP
12:00 N

Prices Su

1960S MENU. The inside of the late 1960s menu from the seafood market at Chris' Restaurant

72

OUR NEW ATTRACTION

Don't leave without stopping by to see our new fish

acquarium containing sharks, king crabs, sea bass flounders,

blow fish, baby fish of all kinds and who knows what else!

★

PLEASE PAY WHEN SERVED

★

SMALL PLATTERS

Small Platters include ONE of the following:
Tartar Sauce, Potato Salad, Cole Slaw or French Fries

10—FRIED OYSTERS	$1.55
11—DEVILED CRAB	1.45
12—DEVILED CLAM	1.30
13—SHRIMP (5)	1.60
14—SCALLOPS (8)	1.40
15—SOFT SHELL CRAB	1.60
16—SCALLOPS (4) and SHRIMP (3)	1.55
17—FLOUNDER	1.35

PIE	30c	COFFEE	15c	
CAKE	25c	TEA	15c	20c
		MILK	15c	20c

E
to 11:30 A.M.
P.M. to 5:30 P.M.

NY
. and 1:00 P.M.

ER
and 7:00 P.M
miles per hour

ILBOAT
A. — 8:30 P.M.
de

UD
P.M.

NG
P.M.

o Change

shows the relatively low prices offered on fresh flounder, clams, and oysters.

CHRIS MONTAGNA WITH FISH. Chris Montagna, pictured above, exhibits a fish he caught. Montagna operated Chris' Restaurant at Ninth Street and Palen Avenue for nearly a half-century. Starting out as a "pound fisherman" operating offshore nets and traps, he built his business into a large operation that included a restaurant, fish market, speedboat rides, and fishing charters.

"ROLLO." Chris Montagna's dog Rollo frequently greeted patrons with his playful antics in the 1950s. (Senior Studio.)

CHRIS' *FLYING SAUCER* BEING LAUNCHED. Billed as the world's fastest passenger speedboat with a top speed of 90 m.p.h., the famed *Flying Saucer* was launched at the Holtz Boatworks in 1953. The boatworks was located on the bayfront between Seventh and Eighth Streets. The *Flying Saucer* was a converted World War II-era P.T. (patrol torpedo) boat 70 feet in length with a 20 foot beam. (Senior Studio.)

FLYING SAUCER AT DOCK. The *Flying Saucer* is pictured here soon after its launching, when it arrived at the dock in front of Chris' Restaurant at Ninth Street and Bay Avenue. (Senior Studio.)

THE *FLYING SAUCER*. The *Flying Saucer* would take up to 125 passengers for an exciting ocean ride. Chris Montagna usually piloted the boat himself. (Senior Studio.)

THE *FLYING PONY*. The *Flying Pony* was one of Chris' first speedboats. Here the speedboat passes under the Ninth Street Bridge during a bayfront parade in the 1950s.

FLYING PONY. The *Flying Pony* is pictured here on one of its speed runs, probably in the mid-1950s. Smaller than the better known *Flying Saucer*, the *Pony*, as it was called by many, proved to be a very popular attraction for speedboat riders who wanted a thrill but not the high speed of the *Flying Saucer*.

THE *SWEETHEART*. The *Sweetheart* was a 65-foot auxiliary sailboat named by Chris Montagna for his wife, Marcia V. Smith. The sailboat took patrons on a two-hour ride into the ocean three times daily at 11:30 am, 2:30 pm, and 8:30 pm.

FLYING CLOUD. One of the fastest fishing boats built for Chris was the *Flying Cloud*, which could attain a speed of 75 m.p.h. This extraordinary fishing boat could take its full capacity of fifty people to the ocean fishing grounds in fifteen minutes. It left Chris' dock daily at 10 am and returned at 3:30 pm.

CHRIS' *GONE WITH THE WIND*. Chris operated several high-speed fishing boats that could get to distant fishing grounds in a matter of minutes. Among the most popular of these charter boats were the *Flying Cloud*, the *Wild Goose*, and the *Gone With The Wind*, pictured here in the late 1950s. Its hull was painted black with white lettering. (Senior Studio.)

THE *WILD GOOSE*. The *Wild Goose* took passengers to deep-sea fishing with lightning speed. Passengers frequently had Chris Montagna himself at the helm of this well-crafted boat. However, the anchor had to be pulled up by hand, thus straining the back of many a young man working with Chris. (Senior Studio.)

TOLEDO SCALE. This old Toledo brand scale on the former Chris' Restaurant docks may date from the heyday of the establishment. The Dockside Cafe now utilizes part of the original site. (F.J. Esposito.)

SOUVENIR PHOTOGRAPH. Mike Cappezza, on the far right, leads a crew of workers peeling shrimp at dockside. The photograph was a souvenir of a visit to Chris' available in the late 1950s. (K.E. Taylor.)

FILETING FISH AT CHRIS'. Leon H. Stowe, right, and Frank Brunetti Jr., second from left, filet flounders at Chris' in the late 1950s. Fried flounder platters were a popular menu item at the restaurant and market.

MIKE CAPPEZZA, *c. 1955.* Mike Cappezza repairs fishing nets on the dock of Chris' Restaurant. Cappezza came from a family reared by the sea. He could re-stitch the nets using traditional methods.

CHRIS' SEAFOOD MARKET. Chris' Seafood Market workers, including manager John J. Esposito, right, prepare clams and flounder at a dockside basin, *c. 1960.*

DOCKSIDE SCENE, 1950s. Mike Cappezza posed for many photographs while demonstrating his seamanship at Chris'. Born on the Italian island of Ischia, Cappezza was Chris' brother-in-law.

CHRIS' DOCKS: CLEANING THE CATCH. Children watch the cleaning of the day's catch at Chris' dock in the early 1960s.

CHRIS' DOCKS: STRAIGHTENING UP. A Chris' worker goes about his task of straightening up the waterfront cafe, c. 1960.

CHRIS' MARKET WORKERS—WOMEN. Chris' Seafood Market and Restaurant waitresses pose for the camera at dockside in the mid 1960s. Seated in the center is Theresa Esposito, manager of the waitresses. The photograph captures the festive atmosphere of the docks at Chris', which were always bedecked with flags and nautical ornamentation.

CHRIS' MARKET WORKERS—MEN. Chris' Seafood Market employed many college students on their summer vacations. The photograph shows manager John J. Esposito (second from left in the rear row) and his youthful employees in the summer of 1970. (Chauvin.)

FOOD PREPARERS AT CHRIS'. The food preparation department for Chris' Restaurant and for the seafood market was photographed in the 1950s in front of the *Flying Saucer* speedboat. Shown are the workers and their supervisor, Mrs. Leon Stowe, (in the second row, fourth from left). Philomena Brunetti (second row, second from left) later became supervisor of the food preparation unit.

CHRIS' WAITRESSES. Chris' waitresses pose for an informal portrait in the early 1960s.

CHRIS' RESTAURANT WAITRESSES AND SUPERVISORS, *c.* 1960. Working at Chris' Restaurant during the summer months proved a pleasant and profitable experience for college-age employees. Many of the students working at Chris' were from Philadelphia-area colleges. They worked as waitresses, waiters, food preparers, and as deck hands on Chris' boats. (Senior Studio.)

NINTH STREET BRIDGE AND BECK'S. For decades, visitors to Ocean City were greeted by the picturesque buildings and docks of Beck's Seafood Restaurant and Chris' Restaurant, both located at the side of the Ninth Street Bridge leading onto the island. The scene is shown here as it appeared in 1936. Beck's Seafood Restaurant, located next door to Chris', was also a very popular dining establishment. Diners had a superb view of the bay from most tables in the second-floor restaurant. Beck's later became Hogate's Restaurant. (Senior Studio.)

HOGATE'S, *c.* 1950s. This bayfront view at Ninth Street shows both Hogate's and Chris' Restaurants in the 1950s. The *Sweetheart* sailboat is in the center of the photograph. A small speedboat named *Marcia* is at the center on Chris' docks. Note Bill's Boat Shop to the right of Chris' Restaurant building. (Senior Studio.)

NINTH STREET BRIDGE. This late 1940s postcard shows both the Ninth Street Bridge and, next to it, the trolley line to the mainland that crossed Great Egg Harbor Bay and entered Ocean City at Eighth Street.

THE DOCKS AT DAN'S SEAFOOD. Dan Montagna (and later his family) operated Dan's Seafood at Tenth Street and the bayfront for many decades. Dan was Chris Montagna's brother. This view from the docks next door reveals the encroachment of recent development along these landmark sites on the bayfront (F.J. Esposito.)

CHRIS MONTAGNA IN RETIREMENT. In his later years Chris Montagna built model boats, went fishing, and cared for his wife and cat. He often reminisced about Chris' Restaurant and his fleet of boats. He passed away in 1987. (Sue Kasunich Matthews.)

OCEAN CITY-LONGPORT BRIDGE. This postcard, mailed in August 1934, showed the "new" Ocean City-Longport Bridge, which first opened a few years earlier in 1928.

OCEAN CITY-LONGPORT BRIDGE IN MIST. This early-morning photograph shows the Ocean City-Longport Bridge clouded in mist. (F.J. Esposito.)

NIGHT IN VENICE PARADE/BAY CARNIVAL. The Night in Venice Parade was fashioned after a similar parade on the bay at the early part of this century called the "Bay Carnival." Here is a decorated boat sailing in the Great Egg Harbor Bay c. 1923. The parade remains a very popular event. (Senior Studio.)

NIGHT IN VENICE PARADE. The annual Night in Venice Parade is held in July along the bayfront. Boats and bayfront homes are decorated with festive lights for the parade. This entry, called "American Made," was in the 1992 parade. (Senior Studio.)

Five
Hurricanes, Storms, and Fires

1944 HURRICANE. The hurricane that directly hit Ocean City on September 14, 1944, caused extensive damage to public structures—including the boardwalk—amounting to over $500,000. Brighton Place, pictured here, was hit extremely hard.

1944 HURRICANE. The hurricane of 1944 destroyed both this house and car near the Fourth Street beach. (Senior Studio.)

1944 HURRICANE—AERIAL VIEW. Bay and ocean waters met in the streets during the 1944 Hurricane. This photograph shows the damage caused between Second Street and Fourth Street with the bay in the foreground.

BEACHFRONT MAYHEM. This house was torn from its foundation by the raging waters of the 1944 Hurricane. A man sits dejectedly on the bumper of a marooned car.

MARCH 1962 STORM—AERIAL VIEW. The March 1962 storm resulted from the rare combination of a full moon, northeast winds, and five unusually high tides. The highest tide of 8.6 feet was only eclipsed by the record 9.0 tide of the 1944 Hurricane. This aerial view is of Tenth Street and West Avenue. The Ocean City Train Station at Tenth Street and Haven Avenue can be seen in the upper center of the photograph.

Left: FOURTEENTH STREET BOARDWALK DAMAGE. Bob's Restaurant at Fourteenth Street and Boardwalk survived the 1962 storm, but the boardwalk in front of it was demolished. Right: BOB'S RESTAURANT. This street-side view shows the damage to the boardwalk and its access ramps as well as to Bob's outdoor hot dog stand, which has vanished.

MARCH 1962 STORM FLOOD WATERS. Flood waters during the 1962 storm damaged or ruined hundreds of cars as streets became totally un-navigable.

DAMAGE TO OCEAN CITY'S SOUTH END. The March 1962 storm wreaked havoc on the modern duplexes in Ocean City's southern end. Here several large buildings have been carried off their foundations by the flood waters.

STORM DAMAGE, 1962. Once-beautiful homes were torn apart by the 1962 storm.

STORM DAMAGE TO OLDER HOMES, 1962. Even older homes could not withstand the fury of this killer storm—one of the century's worst.

STREETS CLOGGED WITH SAND, 1962. The March 1962 storm deposited tons of beach sand throughout the island. It took months for the sand to be totally removed from the streets.

THE BREAKERS HOTEL. The well-known Breakers Hotel was quite literally surrounded by ocean breakers during the 1962 storm.

WIND DAMAGE, 1962. Although high tidal waters did the most severe damage to homes, wind damage removed shingles and downed electric wires in the March 1962 turbulence.

1927 FIRE ON NINTH STREET. The 1927 fire destroyed most of the existing boardwalk and also burned houses in a large area from the boardwalk west to Wesley Avenue. Here, the block between Ocean Avenue and Wesley Avenue on Ninth Street is in ruins. The large building on the right is the Traymore Hotel; the former Ocean City Garage next door was damaged less severely.

FIRE FROM WESLEY AVENUE. This similar view of the aftermath of the 1927 fire also shows the smoldering ruins of buildings between Wesley and Ocean Avenues.

1927 FIRE, WEST ON NINTH STREET. The 1927 fire left a pile of wreckage, as shown in this view from the old boardwalk at Ninth Street looking west.

PLAYLAND FIRE, 1961. A devastating fire in 1961 destroyed the Playland Complex at Sixth Street and Boardwalk, then owned by Howard S. Stainton. The Gillian family today operates Wonderland on the same site. (Senior Studio.)

Scenes of Devastation

THE THREE MILLION DOLLAR FIRE. The 1927 fire devastated a large part of Ocean City.

The damage was estimated at over three million dollars, as this newspaper report revealed.

SILSBY STEAMER. Ocean City initially had a volunteer fire department consisting of three companies. Volunteer firefighters served the community from 1893 to 1930, when city leaders authorized a permanent fire department. The devastating 1927 fire undoubtedly led many to see the need for a permanent department. Pictured here is the horse-drawn Silsby steamer rushing to a fire.

FIRE DEPARTMENT, 1950. The first firehouse, known as Volunteer Company Number 1, stood at the northeast corner of Ninth Street and Asbury Avenue, and was moved to Ninth and West Avenue. Other company firehouses were located at Sixth Street and Asbury Avenue and Twelfth Street and Asbury Avenue. This 1950 photograph shows the members of the permanent fire department on the steps of city hall. (Senior Studio.)

Six
The *Sindia* Shipwreck

SINDIA DECK. In a howling storm in December 1901, the four-masted steel barque *Sindia* came aground at the Sixteenth Street beach. Carrying a cargo of china, camphor oil, and matting, the ship quickly settled in the sand. This shipwreck has captured the imaginations of generations of Ocean City residents. Even today people find small pieces of the steel ship mixed in the shells that wash ashore. This photograph was taken soon after the grounding of the ship. (Senior Studio.)

THE *SINDIA*. When the *Sindia* foundered in the surf, local residents led by Captain J. Mackey Corson saved the entire crew. The ship, en route to New York from Kobe, Japan, came aground in the breakers. It currently rests beneath the sand and has recently been the subject of an officially-sanctioned maritime salvage. (Senior Studio.)

SINDIA FIGUREHEAD. The figurehead from the *Sindia* was a representation of a leader of the Scindia family of the Indian province of Gualior. This head portion of what was originally a full-body figurehead is now on display at the Ocean City Historical Museum located at 1735 Simpson Avenue.

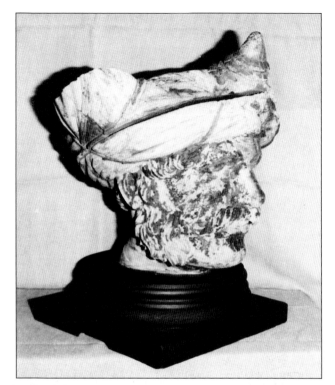

TAKING CARGO FROM "SINDIA"

TAKING CARGO OFF THE *SINDIA*. Salvagers, including a diver, are shown here removing a part of the valuable cargo *c.* 1905. Now greatly prized by collectors, *Sindia* china sold for only a few cents after a partial salvage of the ship's cargo.

SINDIA AT SAIL. The *Sindia* sailed from Kobe, Japan, and was bound for New York City when it met its fate on Ocean City's beach.

SINDIA WRECK. The wreck of the *Sindia* is shown here beginning to sink into the sands.

SINDIA WITH DECKS AWASH. In this 1902 photograph, waves are crashing across the ship's deck. The masts and riggings are still in place. Through the years, the metal hull of the *Sindia* has probably protected the large cargo still on the ship. An unsuccessful salvage, attempted more than a decade ago, resulted in a barge breaking loose from its moorings near the *Sindia* and then crashing into the Fourteenth Street fishing pier. Although organizers abandoned that salvage attempt, there is still hope among some that a new effort will shed some light on the mystery surrounding the disaster, as well as provide priceless artifacts for study. (Senior Studio.)

SINDIA THEN AND NOW. The *Sindia* wreck has long been a popular subject for postcards from Ocean City.

THE OLD WRECK. This 1923 postcard shows one of the *Sindia*'s masts still standing more than twenty years after the disaster.

EARLY SNAPSHOT OF *SINDIA* WRECKAGE. A mast, tiller, and parts of the hull are visible in this early-twentieth-century photograph. The *Sindia* wreckage has been clearly visible on a few occasions during this century. It rests on the grave of at least one other shipwreck at the same site. (Senior Studio.)

SINDIA WRECK. A remarkable blowout tide exposed the outline and framework of the *Sindia* for a short time in February 1985. (Senior Studio.)

SINDIA CHINA. The Ocean City Historical Museum at 1735 Simpson Avenue has on display excellent examples of *Sindia* china. Local residents salvaged some of the china or bought it from the *Sindia* store, which was selling this beautifully-colored china at bargain prices by today's standards.

HULL OF *SINDIA*, 1985. A portion of the hull of the *Sindia* was uncovered during this unique 1985 tidal phenomenon. (Senior Studio.)

Seven
Famous Residents

KELLY HOME. The John B. and Margaret Kelly family owned this home at Twenty-sixth Street and Wesley Avenue for many years. Here, Grace, Jack Jr., Lizanne, and Peggy spent their summers enjoying Ocean City and its pristine white beaches. The Kelly children would frequently bring soda and sandwiches to the lifeguards on the Twenty-sixth Street beach. Jack Jr., known as "Kell," first served as a mascot and then later as a member of the Ocean City Beach Patrol.

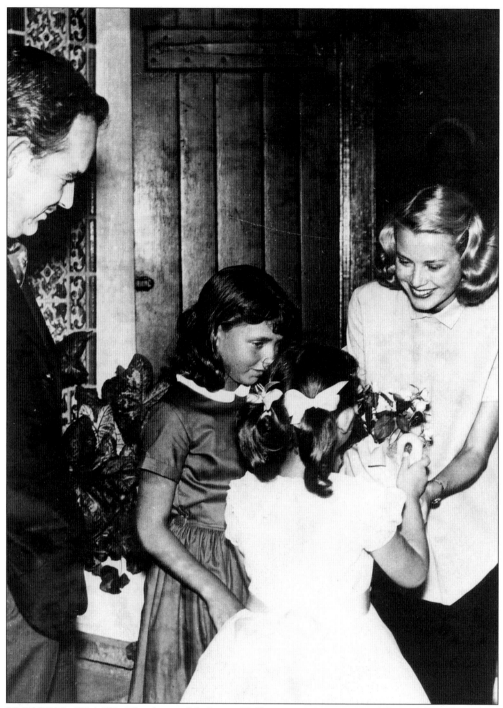

PRINCESS GRACE. The beautiful Grace Kelly was a very successful model and motion picture actress before she married Prince Ranier of Monaco in 1956. Here she is accepting flowers from two girls in Ocean City as the prince looks on. Princess Grace died in a tragic automobile accident in France on September 14, 1982. She remains a greatly-loved figure in Ocean City.

JOHN B. KELLY SR. John B. Kelly Sr. was an Olympic oarsman from Philadelphia who took his family, including daughter Grace and son John B. Jr. (also a champion Olympic sculler), to Ocean City for summer vacations. The senior Kelly won gold medals in both the 1920 and 1924 Olympics.

MRS. MARGARET KELLY AND DAUGHTERS. Mrs. Margaret Kelly (center) and daughters Peggy (left), Grace, and Lizanne (right) pose together in the 1950s in Ocean City.

Created to commemorate the favorable impact the family of John B. & Margaret ~ Kelly have had in developing Ocean City ~ N.J. ~ into ~ America's Greatest Family Resort

Presented ~ Ocean City Historical Museum April 10-'83 Jack Jr. ~ Lizanne ~ Peggy and Princess Grace (in Spirit)

Made by T. John Carey
Ocean City - N.J.

"I would like to be remembered as a decent human being and a caring one"
Princess Grace, July 22, 1982

OCEAN CITY HISTORICAL MUSEUM
409 Wesley Avenue
Ocean City, New Jersey
"Sindia" wrecked on 16th Street beach at Ocean City, New Jersey, December 15th, 1901. She sailed from Japan, headed for New York City. It became a New Jersey State Historical Site in 1967.

4/10/83
best wishes
Albert di Monaco

MOMENTO: KELLY CEREMONY, 1983. On April 10, 1983, Ocean City honored the memory of the late Princess Grace in a special tribute at the Music Pier. The large image above shows a photograph momento created by Elizabeth Carey and distributed by the Hostess Committee of the historical museum (the plaque pictured was fashioned by T. John Carey). The inset (right) shows a postcard signed by Princess Grace's son, Prince Albert, who was present at the ceremonies.

116

GAY TALESE. Gay Talese, one of America's finest writers, is Ocean City's most famous literary figure. Raised in Ocean City, Talese still maintains a home here. Among his best known works are *Honor Thy Father*, *The Kingdom and the Power*, and *Thy Neighbor's Wife*. All were best-selling books.

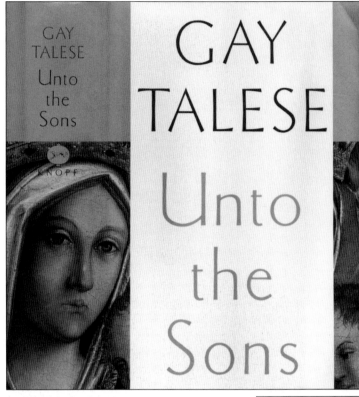

FORMER TALESE STORE AND HOME.
This store at 744 Asbury Avenue is now
housed in the building that served first as the
Talese Tailor Shop and later as the Talese
Clothing Store. The upstairs apartment was
Gay Talese's childhood home.

E.E. HALLERAN. E.E. Halleran was an Ocean City High School history teacher who also doubled as a writer of popular western adventure stories. His paperback westerns reached the peak of their popularity in the 1950s and 1960s.

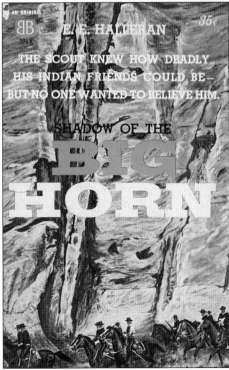

BOOK COVER: HALLERAN BOOK. Published in 1960 by Ballantine Books, Halleran's *Shadow of the Big Horn* depicted the tension between American Indians and newly-arrived white settlers. He oftentimes portrayed the Indian characters in his stories with a special sensitivity.

THOMAS "TOMMY" LEE. A 1954 graduate of Ocean City High School, "Tommy" Lee became one of the nation's top thoroughbred horse jockeys in a twenty-year racing career that began in 1957. A popular jockey who won often at New Jersey, Delaware, and Maryland racetracks, he amassed over fifteen hundred wins in his career including several major stakes races. In 1964 he won the Maryland jockey championship with 169 wins, thus topping all riders at Laurel, Pimlico, and Bowie racetracks. An injury ended his riding career in 1977 but he remains close to racing and is currently Clerk of the Scales for the state of Maryland.

CONGRESSMAN WILLIAM J. HUGHES. Congressman William J. Hughes, shown here in 1989, represented the second congressional district for over twenty years. A resident of Ocean City, Hughes was best known in Congress as an articulate spokesperson for maritime and resort-related issues. The highly-regarded political leader first came to office when he upset incumbent Charles W. Sandman in 1974. In 1995 he was appointed United States ambassador to Panama by President Bill Clinton. (*Ocean City Sentinel-Ledger*/Fitzpatrick.)

CHARLES W. SANDMAN AND GERALD FORD. Hughes defeated Charles W. Sandman, pictured here with President Gerald Ford, in the congressional races of 1974. Sandman was known during the Watergate era as a staunch defender of Richard Nixon. Even though he didn't live in Ocean City, Sandman was an influential figure here. He represented the community in both the state senate and in the United States House of Representatives. (*Ocean City Sentinel-Ledger.*)

CONGRESSMAN WILLIAM J. HUGHES AND DORIS MARTS. In 1989, then-Congressman Hughes received an award from the Ocean City Historical Museum that was presented to him by Doris Marts, curator of the museum and the owner of Senior Studio. (*Ocean City Sentinel-Ledger.*)

Eight
Epilogue

COMMUNITY CENTER. The Ocean City Community Center, built in 1979, provides a varied range of activities for residents and visitors. The center, located at 1735 Simpson Avenue, houses the Ocean City Historical Museum, an aquatic and fitness center, and the local library.

BED AND BREAKFAST RESTORATIONS. The Northwood Inn at 401 Wesley Avenue is a beautifully-restored Victorian-era inn. It is located in Ocean City's recently-designated historic district. (F.J. Esposito.)

SCOTCH HALL. Scotch Hall, located at 435 Wesley Avenue, served as the home of Ezra B. Lake, one of the town's founders. It has served various functions since then as a hospital, a convalescent home, and now, as a restaurant.

MAYOR TROFA. Mayor Nickolas J. "Chick" Trofa was an ardent defender of the unique historical and traditional character of Ocean City. His sudden death while in office shocked and saddened the community. This commemorative plaque is at the Music Pier on the boardwalk.

BAYSIDE CENTER. The former Wheaton Estate at Sixth Street and bayfront will be operated by the City of Ocean City as a historic site following the purchase of this landmark by the county government. This aerial view of the estate in April 1952 shows the estate building (above right) and a neighboring building as the only structures on the bayfront between Fifth and Sixth Streets. (Senior Studio.)

SEASHORE COTTAGE. The Seashore Cottage at 1139 Wesley Avenue is owned and operated by the Friends of the Ocean City Historical Museum and furnished as a typical seaside cottage of the 1920s through 1940s. The Hobo Fountain can be seen at the bottom right of the photograph. (Senior Studio.)

NINTH STREET BRIDGE. The crossing of the Ninth Street Bridge is the final leg of any trip over the causeway from the mainland to the barrier island of Ocean City and its many unique cultural, historical, and recreational attractions. (F.J. Esposito.)

1940S OCEAN CITY BILLBOARD. In her 1895 Ocean City guidebook, Mary Townsend Rush described the island community in colorful terms: "Down to it's shores flock invalids, worn and weary with the burden of the body; school children, white and wan; and businessmen nerves unstrung and shattered. Nature lays her hand upon her children and restores waning strength to the weary body, paints the white face with the ruddy hue of health, looses the tension, and soothes into an indescribable peace and rest the overtaxed nerves." People continue to come to Ocean City—over one hundred years later—for many of the same comforts that inspired this 1895 writer. This 1940s billboard stood at the corner of Route 9 and the Somers Point-Mays Landing Road. It proclaimed what still is Ocean City's proud slogan: "America's Greatest Family Resort." (Senior Studio.)

Bibliography

Cain, Tim. *Peck's Beach: A Pictorial History of Ocean City*. Harvey Cedars: Down The Shore Publishing, 1988.

Cunningham, John T. *The New Jersey Shore*. New Brunswick: Rutgers University Press, 1958.

Esposito, Frank J. *Travelling New Jersey*. Union City: William Wise, 1978.

Lamphear, Alberta, compiler. *The Saga of The* Sindia, *December 15, 1901*. Ocean City: Ocean City Historical Museum, 1992.

Lee, Harold. *A History of Ocean City*. Ocean City: Friends of the Ocean City Historical Museum, 1965.

Lee, Harold. *Ocean City Memories*. Ocean City: Centennial Commission, 1979.

Roberts, Russell and Rich Youmans. *Down The Jersey Shore*. New Brunswick: Rutgers University Press, 1993.

Rush, Mary Townsend. *Ocean City Guidebook and Directory*. Ocean City: 1892-95.

Seibold, David J. and Charles J. Adams III. *Shipwrecks off Ocean City*. Wyomissing Hills, Pennsylvania: D. Seibold, 1986.

Wilson, Harold F. *The Jersey Shore*. New York: Lewis Publishing Company, 1953. Also Van Nostrand, 1964.